Colorful

the woman. the wife. the mother.

DEBORAH C. ANTHONY

Unless otherwise indicated, all scripture quotations, references and definitions are from the Authorized King James Version © 1987; The New King James Version © 1982 by Thomas Nelson, Inc.; The New International Version 1973, 1978, 1984 by International Bible Society by the Zondervan Corporation; The Amplified Bible Old Testament © 1962, 1964, 1965, 1987 by the Zondervan Corporation; The Amplified New Testament © 1954, 1958, 1987 by the Lockman Foundation; The Message. Copyright © 1993, 1994, 1995, 1996, 2000, 2001, 2002. Used by permission of NavPress Publishing Group. All rights reserved; M.G. Easton M.A., D.D., Illustrated Bible Dictionary, Third Edition, published by Thomas Nelson, 1897; The Name Book © 1982, 1997 by Dorothy Astoria.

COLORFUL
The Woman - The Wife - The Mother

Deborah C. Anthony
info@deborahcanthony.com
www.deborahcanthony.com

Copyright © 2019 Deborah C. Anthony
ISBN: 978-1-943343-01-0

Published by
PublishAffordably.com | 773.783.2981 | Chicago, Illinois

Dedication

To the woman who taught me how to love color on every level. I would walk into her presence, and there she was with her bright orange hat and t-shirt. I will never forget her orange Air Force Ones. Nina-Marie Leslie, you exude the very fiber of love and color. I would walk into your bathroom in your home and say to myself, *"One day when I grow up, I will have all of these colors in my bathroom."*

Your unique anointing and presence were always met with colorful things that made you happy. As I stood in your living room, I remember you saying to me, *"Daughter, you will write the book **The Woman - The Wife - The Mother** because Father God is perfecting you in all areas."*

You decided to go and be with the Glory Cloud, and now I press on to begin to fulfill just a measure of what you sowed into my life. Nina-Marie, you taught me to give grace, to love everybody, to never quit because

Calvary did not quit on me. I stand now in juxtaposition, holding onto that very promise God has spoken over my life through you. I say thank you for the countless years of special coffee, family movie nights, and pouring into my family a love only a mom could give.

Your life represents a colorful life full of joy and full of the majestic glory of God. Thank you for teaching me that those that suffer with Him will reign with Him. Mama Nina, you will always be forever the lady with those red lipstick kisses and the love that forever grows in my heart.

I love you from here to Heaven, forever colorful.

Love,
Deborah

-Willie Aurelia Irwin-

Foreword

For many, Sunday is a day of rest, but for me it is a day set aside to serve God. Mary Mary's song "Sunday Morning" perfectly expresses the anticipation that I feel every week, as I countdown the weekdays until it is Sunday morning. Church is the place where we praise God through singing songs, listening to the Word, and where we worship by lifting our hands. And of course, we wear our "Sunday's best."

The Sunday I met Deborah, she had checked off all the Sunday morning boxes. She was praising God, lifting her holy hands, and her "Sunday's best" reflected her financial success. Her suit and shoes were so bad; the kind of "bad" that indicated her impeccable taste, and flare for fashion. Although Deborah appeared to be successful, her genuine desire to please God was what was most striking and undeniable.

I have had the privilege of witnessing Deborah's evolution as a woman of God. He has perfected her through the challenges of life, and He has promoted her time after time. I have seen God move miraculously in her life as she has passionately pursued His Heart, and His purpose. To share the story of God's grace in your life, requires transparency and a heart that will bare itself, so that someone else may find the freedom to discover God's purpose for their lives.

In this book, you will find a vessel that was far from perfect but has been fully transformed through an uncompromising desire and commitment to serving God. "Colorful - The Woman/The Wife/ The Mother" is Deborah's life testimony of profound examples of God's grace. My daughter in Christ has tapped into a place that drives women to experience renewal and new beginnings; a place where women can truly discover God's purpose in their lives.

Table of Contents

Chapter Three

The Mother Who Is *Colorful*

Chapter Four

Chosen For The *Journey*

Introduction

The word **illusion** can be defined as *"a thing that is or is likely to be wrongly perceived or interpreted by the senses. Any promise of utter certitude or satisfaction is an illusion."*

The problem is, we try to relate to a God that promises to make us certain and satisfy all of our desires through an illusion, an idol. If we chase the idol, we find that one of two things will ultimately happen. Either we fail to get the things we really want, resulting in depression and/or sadness; or we do succeed and discover that success cannot deliver what we truly desire, also resulting in depression and/or sadness. Then we wonder why there are so many sad and depressed people in this world.

Little girls are often shaped by the many ideas and thoughts of what they imagine their lives could be like. Many of our ideas come from hurts wrought from our life experiences. We begin to shape and build this idea of what we want our lives to be. Some of our fairy tale ideations come from how we saw our parents live. We either embrace that concept or we reject it.

As I share the journey of the last 40-plus years of my life, I realize I have evolved or one might say "morphed" into a woman of many colors and facets.

I want to share with you who I believed I was vs. who I am today. A mentor asked me a question many years ago - **Who are you?** That question puzzled me because I thought she knew of all my accomplishments. I *repeated* everything that I felt I had built for my life from a college education to a great job and countless other successes. At that point, I didn't realize that my validation came solely from what I perceived to be success. It was then I began to see that I had built various illusions, perceptions, and even versions of who I believed I was.

Most of us have an idea that we either believed or told ourselves concerning what our life is, in order to cope through life's various trials and circumstances. I had no idea when the question was posed to me, *"Who are you"*, that it would be the beginning of a pursuit toward real identity and authenticity.

As I write today, I share the many tears, the many joys, and the lessons of my journey. I have come to know, we truly have only one life, and we must seize every moment, living each day to make it all count. We cannot allow the past, be it victories, failures, or even illusions to hold us hostage from moving forward. Illusions hold us hostage because we only want to see ourselves in the light of what we want to believe. Seeing ourselves in our truest form will cause us to have to face not our challenges now, but our past hurts as well. We must keep moving forward, no matter what it takes.

Early in my journey I created coping mechanisms to get through my life. At the age of 12, I walked into a flower shop, down the street from my childhood home, and asked the owner for a job. One would say that was pretty ambitious or self-driven for me. Perhaps the little girl in me was starting to escape from her daily reality to begin painting a picture of who I really wanted to be.

Throughout this book, you will read a lot about *"the painting."* The painting is the picture you paint for yourself with brush strokes of your own colors and images that you want to see things as. It is the beginning of shaping an illusion of what you want your life to be.

When I was a little girl, I would always draw a picture of a house with four windows, a fence with flowers all around the house, and a bright shining sun tucked up in the corner of the page. I was never a good artist, so my drawings featured a stick-figure family standing together in front of the house. As I grew older, that picture became an oil painting of who I was going to be , which I wrapped up in my goals of, *"By this age, I will have done this,"* and *"By this age, I will have this many degrees,"* and so on.

As you read through my journey, I want you to imagine your life unplanned and unscripted. I challenge you to bring along no preconceived notions of who you believe you are. Imagine what your life would look like if you allowed the Creator to be the artist and just let Him put His image on your canvas. Would there be less trials, less hurt, less to cry about? Or has this ability that God gave us to choose His life disappeared in you? We don't always make the right choice, but God even uses our everyday moments to teach us, grow us, and give us the gift of helping someone else along the way.

So as I shared, as I got older, in this painting, I became driven by what I could accomplish and worked very hard at making declarative statements like "I don't want to be like…" "I will have this…" "I am going to have my own…." I was so determined to fight against the ideas that I saw others live through, that sometimes I clipped at my own growth and missed out on having some amazing relationships and life experiences.

I am number five among my eight siblings and have always tried to be just as mature as they were, completely avoiding the experience of acting like a child or having childlike behaviors like playing with dolls. Playing with children my age was a no-no. I didn't realize that with this behavior I was rejecting an experience to be a child and live out my childhood. My mother tried to get me to join the Girl Scouts and be with other children my age. I rejected those ideas and attempts to salvage my childhood. Instead, I was always living 10 steps ahead of myself and constantly desiring something that was so far in front of me that I missed out on living in the moment and truly experiencing the stage of life I was actually in.

This caused me to further create on my canvas images that I was not ready for—images that I didn't have the experience to support that stage of life. Instead of successfully painting every picture, I would come to a place where I was really drawing the various stages of a woman's journey as an illusion. I would try to be who I believed I was in that perfect picture in my mind vs. the canvas the Creator intended from the beginning of time, one that I kept rejecting.

That question, *"Who are you?"* was on July 15, 2009, 15 days after I was fired from my corporate job. It forced me to see the of image of myself that I didn't want to let go of. Let's take a look.

COLORFUL

Chapter One

The Woman

Woman, you are colorful.
Your smile, your experience, your shape.
Woman, you are chosen!

Deborah

COLORFUL

Who Are You?

Who I Am . . .

I am now a woman of God that has truly embraced all that comes with being me. I stand firmly centered in knowing that I have been redeemed. I can be very comical at times, yet extremely focused at other times. I am not afraid to look in the mirror with all that comes with being me. I am a task master, driven, an exciting, and loving person—that is who I am. I no longer choose to identify myself with things and people, but I now make a conscious decision to be whole in the One who I was created to be. I am constantly chasing after Him to become like Him.

I am the woman who owns what I look like; because it is all a part of who I am. As I continue in this season of maturation, I am encouraged to write and share the many places of change and healing in my life. As I am writing, I am experiencing some residue of brokenness, but I am also honestly recognizing that in my perceived weakness, God is strong, and that is what truly matters. At one point in my life, I thought I was very good at details, but I see that God wants me to look a little closer at those areas that I sometimes overlooked. Although I am whole, I am grateful for those times in my life where I couldn't see God's imprint on my life, because they brought me to Him.

What I Do . . .

I can truly say that this question used to be easier to answer. I mean I could ramble off who I thought I was to anyone. Five roles come to mind:

I am:
- An entrepreneur/business owner
- A mother of six
- A wife to a handsome husband
- A CEO of a non-profit organization
- A woman of GOD—wait, make that a MIGHTY woman of God ☺

All of those powerful areas that I thought defined me really are not as important as WHO I AM. I appreciate all that I am able to do, but it is not WHO I AM.

In this season of my life, I have discovered roles are temporal in the eyes of God. That does not take away from the great responsibility that each one of us has or the weight that comes with each. It is so important to ascertain a balance in our make-up because each part of us makes up WHAT I DO. I often take many deep breaths and ask the Lord, "*How shall I do WHAT I DO?*"

One day, the light bulb came on and I realized that I cannot do anything without God, not even the smallest thing of my life.

So now WHAT DO I DO? I sit waiting for instruction, asking the Father what His daily plan is for me. He has a plan and a will for my life and all I have to do is rest and do just what He says. I do what He has called me to do and only that. I will not run around creating things to do. I will not lean into my intellect or understanding, but I consciously seek Him for what His plan is for my life.

The quest for *The WOMAN, The WIFE, The MOTHER* began with the question "WHO ARE YOU?" As you read this book, I pray that you will find yourself in whatever stage you are in, realizing that you will evolve, you will grow, and certainly will be stretched. You will feel as though you are dying and beg to be rescued from yourself. Staying the course is so critical. You must understand, there is only one you. There is only one blueprint that God has designed for your life and you must walk in purpose and destiny to fulfill the promises that are on your life.

The Woman
"I can become the woman
or I can just be the woman."
Deborah

Dreams

Everything in our lives begins with a dream or an idea; something we imagined or something we saw and said, "I want that." *The Cosby Show* was instrumental in shaping the possibility in me that, *"I can have it all as a woman, wife, and mother."* Although it was a television show, it caused me to dream about having success and having it all in one episode.

In this life, we all have this dream of who we want to become when we grow up. In school, on many occasions, one of the questions I was asked was, *"Who do you want to be when you grow up?"* One might respond with *"A doctor, lawyer, police officer, or a teacher."* Those were the typical answers that I heard among my peers. It was interesting however, I did not hear much discussion or interest in being a mom, a wife, or even a homemaker. Marriage and family may have been assumed, but not regarded as a career choice.

As a young girl, I wanted to be a businesswoman. I will never forget at the tender age of 10, I saw the DeVry Institute of Technology commercial on television. I called the number and said I wanted information, not even knowing enough about what that looked like. They were kind enough to ask me to call back when I graduated from high school.

Sometimes, our dreams are shaped by our natural abilities and sometimes they are shaped by that driving force that lies within those who are strong, determined, and self-driven. As I shared in the introduction, at age 12, I started my first job at a flower shop. By age 14, I was working for a dental office processing claims. By age 16, I was working for a bank as a teller.

It was at these moments that my ideals and world views, as well as certain idiosyncrasies were being shaped by my environment. The dream to become "somebody" was birthed in those experiences. My dream of no longer struggling was emerging from coming from a large family where you have to share everything and learn to go without, which I hated. So, I took out my paint brush and began to create a dream on the canvas of my life.

The "Woman" is such a huge piece to this story because she has such creative power. The challenge was for her not to go outside of God's plan or outside of the boundaries that He purposed from the foundations of the world.

Career

Needless to say, ambition was not an issue in my life. My eyes were so big at a young age to pursue a career. I was never sure of what profession I ultimately wanted to be in, but I always knew I wanted to be a corporate leader. Working in the banking industry at such a young age, caused me to always want to have money and lots of it. Like every little girl, I was told to graduate from high school, go to college, and pursue a career. Yet, I graduated from high school without a solid plan.

It was June of 1995 and there was nothing in sight for my educational future. My mother (thank God for her) said, *"I am taking you to DeVry to register for school,"* which started in July. There would be no break, no time to question any other option. The picture at this stage in my life was painted as usual—in a hurry. I realized I had always felt RUSHED. Rushing to achieve. Rushing to understand. Rushing through shame. Rushing, but still with dreams. I was always on a mission to get somewhere, to do something, but I did not enjoy the young life that I had been given. I'm not exactly sure, but I suspect that my life's circumstances and trials had forced me to live in such a rushed, survival mode that I lived an abbreviated lifestyle.

The college degree I pursued had a focus on business operations centered on manufacturing, which would adjust to any type of facility or logistics industry. I had no passion for this, but I knew that I loved being in charge of something. In my interview with my first job, they asked me, *"So why do you want this job?"* My response at the tender age of 20 years old was, *"I love telling people what to do."* All I saw were dollar signs. At 20 years old, being offered $50k? I thought it was amazing and unheard of. Not paying attention to what I would be doing and what it would require of me, I blindly said "yes".

I knew the picture I had created for myself was brush-stroked with bright-green dollar signs. I was not looking at what that experience would cost me in the long run. And I certainly had not considered what part of my life I had traded.

For some of you, you may be at the point where you are still in college and have no clue as to where you are going or what you plan to do with your life. I was not that kind of girl. I was so ambitious—eyes wide open, determined to climb out of the pits of poverty. I was not caring about who I disregarded or hurt to accomplish my goals. And although I applaud that little girl who was so full of ambition, I want to caution any 20-year-old, or for that matter, any career-focused woman to never allow your dreams, ambitions, or career goals to be so big that you push out the most valuable assets God has given you.

Those first assets would be faith, family, and friends. You can move through life just as easily with those things intact. At the naïve age of 20, I had no idea what I was doing. I had a focus on a painting that I had begun which was called "**By Any Means Necessary.**" The problem with this is that you will miss and overlook so many moments that are critical to your success. You will be driven, not by moral standards or principles, but by your own goals and selfish wants, you see survival as essential. This is a critical life lesson, never sacrifice your values at the altar of your ambition. I earned and learned this through painful experience.

Beginning this journey, as I did, caused me to become the "SHORT-CUT" queen. Learning to maneuver around and always find the shortest way to get to a goal was both my tactical and strategic plan. I finished what should have taken a four-year bachelor's degree in two and a half years. I advanced on the job with promotion after promotion. The focus of family was there, but later on, you will read about my life as the "wife" and the "mother." I always had them in my self-painted portrait, but at that stage in my life, it was the career that came first.

As I share about my career, I must say that it did shape me into a pretty savvy businesswoman, so not all of the journey was a waste. To every strong, ambitious girl out there I say, *"Plow forward and keep your head up high!"* I also circumspectly advise and inquire you to consider at this point in your journey, **"WHO ARE YOU?"** This question will be the resounding statement as you read on because this one question will help shape your every decision, your every moment, how you treat people, how you love, and how you give.

The art of survival will only take you so far in life. At some point in your journey in life, you have to begin to really LIVE, not just exist. You will need to choose to take the life lessons and live them out, producing the precious fruit that others can live off of and glean from. All success is not good success. As women, we are often willing to sacrifice it all to get to what we want; but we should pause long enough to count the cost of the time and effort that we put in.

Who I Wanted to Be

Let me tell you who I wanted to be. I wanted to be the girl with the corner office on the 15th floor, looking out on Chicago's Michigan Avenue. Instead, I was the girl walking the lines of a cookie and snack factory telling people what to do. *How did I get here?* I asked myself many times. I didn't know how far off I was from who I wanted to be, but the golden handcuffs of the almighty dollar was enough at that time for me. Having money became enough for me to continue trading my real career dreams and desires for what power I thought I had instead.

When you dream about the person you want to be, it is all relative to what stage in life you find yourself. I had traded in the "office dream" for the dollar amount in my bank account. I had painted a picture to the outside world that I have this big-time job. I was going to buy my own place, move out of my mother's house, and so on and so forth. Truth be told, I did do all of the things I said to become who I wanted to be.

However, it is this word that comes with trouble. **INDEPENDENCE**. I wanted to prove to everyone that I could handle everything on my own. In this, the problem becomes you can spend a lifetime imprisoned by another powerful but troublesome word—**PROVE**. Trying to keep up and maintain becomes like bands of chains because you always have others in mind as the motivation behind why you do things.

So who I wanted to be, or have others see me as, was this young, black, successful girl—the girl that everyone would admire and aspire to be like because I fought so hard through many challenges just to be "that" girl in the painting of this picture, However, along the way I regretfully hurt many people trying to be who I wanted to be.

PURE TRUTH MOMENT: We can miss out on the important stuff in life trying to be who we want vs. living in the moment that God has given us and pursuing His purpose and timing. We can be head-strong, short-sided, and in full pursuit of something that even though attainable is not even what we want deep down.

The word "**independent**" means freedom from or no longer being dependent on someone or something. The underlying issue with this is that in life, it is almost impossible to live without being dependent on something or someone. Life, however, does not tell you that, at first. I wanted to be someone on my own, free from parents and anything that looked like control. This was, of course, the mindset of a young woman who had no clue that life would make them dependent on many things. Just give it time.

So on this journey of who I wanted to be, it took me straight to reality where I painted a picture that was reflective of who I thought I was. No longer was it showing me who I wanted to be, but it made me convince myself of who I really was.

Who I Thought I Was

Funny story. One of my best friends and sisters would make fun of me because I was so proud of myself for having purchased my own car. My first car was a sea-green Ford Contour with an 11% interest rate. At the time, I had no idea that was high. I got up in front of the entire church and shared my testimony of what God did for me. I shamed my family by saying no one in my family had good enough credit to help me sign for the car and that I did it all on my own. Talk about stupid! *WHO DID IT THINK I WAS?* I was an arrogant, simple little 20-year-old who had not lived long enough to understand what I was saying or even realize the impact of my words. I painted another picture of myself. Let me share the picture with you, so you can see really clearly the "WHO" I thought I was. It goes a little like this...

I was a college graduate with my own condo and my own car, who lived by myself, making 50k plus a year, who did all of this on my own. I didn't need anyone because I could do it all myself, and my family had nothing to do with how I got there. My family was dysfunctional. My mom and dad had divorced. My brothers and sisters were all over the place. In my mind, I saw them different from me because a few of them were married and some were just in their own world. But no one was as successful as me because I was a fighter. I made it out of the poverty cycle, and I was on the top of the world. Mind you, I was working in a cookie factory. My dream job was a corner office on the 15th floor; except my corner office was hot, smelly, and far from Michigan Avenue. But no one knew on the outside. Even though my situation was not ideal. I had my own place, right? I had my own car but no friends. But that did not matter. I had created an idea in my head of who I thought I was, and I went with it.

So this girl grew into a woman. And well, that canvas continued by painting a picture of the wife I thought I was, to becoming the mother I believed I was. Those stories you will read later in this book, but I have to pause to tell you about the reality that process caused. For the picture of who I thought I was, was simply an illusion built on the pure frustration of the life I thought I deserved vs. the life God had given me.

When you have experienced life's trials and disappointments, you tend to build a life of illusion around WHO you think you are. That idea will only take you so far and will only lead you to a dead end. Dead ends result in having no peace or joy. Nothing really makes you happy or fulfilled. It does not even begin to scratch the surface of what you are truly longing for.

I realized on this journey who I thought I was, was not real at all. It was something I had built to survive and to cope with the many disappointments life had brought. Trying to be authentic with others is not even possible because you truly don't know whether you are being true or real. You actually find yourself manipulating circumstances and people to work for you. The purpose of this moment is to come clean and be honest. To check out your motives and really re-evaluate: *Why do I do what I do? Why do I say the things I say? Why are these people in my life?* This was the beginning of the next part of my journey, which started with a hard question, Who *does God say that I am?* That became the most important question of my lifetime. The hardest part of this process, however, was taking ownership for who I was not.

Ask yourself this: *Do you have people in your life that will be honest with you?* People like my sister, who years later came to me saying," Hey *you know you hurt our family the day you got up in front of the church and said no one had good credit, thinking you were sharing this amazing story, yet hurting everyone you love."* At that moment, I broke inside because of how many times I had hurt others to make myself feel great or significant. It was probably more than I can count and certainly more than I would want to admit.

In my remorse, I began the journey of who God says I am, which started a lifetime of seeking and pursuing Him…

Who He says I Am

It's amazing the time and care that God put into creating the first women—Eve. It speaks volumes to the process that it takes for a baby to develop in a mother's womb. The woman's role is vital not only to the reproduction of life, but also to the development and purposes of that life. All of us as women either have the story where someone did their job so well in our lives that we were so confident and assured that we really didn't need God in our lives. Or, the opposite occurred where we lived a life with no one affirming our purpose and became one who was constantly seeking and gravitating toward something that would help us feel worthy. It took me 40-plus years on earth to reach the place where **I Now**

I Believe I Am Worthy
For I Am Who He (The Father), Says That I Am

I stand firm in God with all my failures, all my struggles, even in all my victories, in all my experiences. In all that was given to me—the good, the bad, and the ugly—I see the love of Father God's hands all over my life. The challenge in this place as a woman, is that many of us reject the vehicle that God wants to use to change our lives. We find something wrong with everything that happens in our lives, never finding the true joy in our weakness and letting His strength be made perfect.

Yes, at times, life sucks but the WOMAN must arise to the occasion with her flawed canvas, full of her ideas and beliefs, and lay them all down at the Master's feet. I can say that the WOMAN in me has learned to just BE; to simply give in to His chosen plan for my life. I also have to say that the painting I drew 30 years ago as a little girl looks a lot different now, and the painting I created 20 years ago looks very shallow in comparison to the life I now have.

As I wrote *"Fully Surrendered"* I once again turned over all my art supplies and canvases to the One that created me. I let Him speak words of life and love over my life and that let me know it was going to all work out. He assured me that I did not need to look to anyone but Him—that HE's GOT ME. Thinking about that makes me say, "Wow!" Most of us search our entire lives for a person to give that type of security, wanting them to say, *"Hey, I GOT YOU, and I will never leave you or forsake YOU."*

Don't allow life circumstances to whisper and chip away at that voice of confidence in you. Before you can give to this world, you must know that this **woman** in you is ready; that she is strong, she is brave, and she is full of grace and love. You don't have to stay in a place of looking for something outside of yourself to be fulfilled. I did that for so many years, juggling my career, having friends, earning money, and even getting married. The **woman** is always in search of her next suitor who will say, *"Hey I GOT YOU."*

Others of us might rush right over the man and continue to plow and plow. At the end of the day, we are so empty. We may make the mistake of running right to the altar for marriage, bringing our half, instead of our whole. Marriage is not 50/50. It is 100/100, two complete individuals coming together as one. Your situation may not even be marriage. It could involve indulging in food, or pouring yourself into your children, or your career. Every one of us has that thing that causes us to lose sight of our true purpose, attempting to satisfy a place in us through something other than God's design.

Our God uses everything. He wastes none of our past, our present, or our future. God desires to affirm us and to complete the woman that dwells within.

She's Real? (Authentic)

In the nineties, there was a saying, *"Keeping it real."* That phrase gave permission to the next statement that would fly out of a person's mouth, no matter how harsh or cruel. But, the problem with keeping it real is that the statement made was only based on how you felt in that moment. The danger in feelings is that they fluctuate, especially in women. So today, it is not about keeping it real with ourselves, or real with your girlfriends. It is time to be real with God.

As a woman, letting our hair down and being free from all the opinions of others, it seems impossible to do. But through this book, this canvas, I hope you will see yourself and say, "I'M REAL" and challenge yourself to become honest and find your true self. Let's start from where you are right now and build a life of truth, which allows for the mistakes but also allows for the learning and growth that only comes from making mistakes.

The things in this life that can be so hard are maintaining relationships with others. You can do your best and even think you're doing a good job but at the end of the day, you still may fail that good friend or disappoint that loved one. In my *"keeping it real"* moment, God remained constant. Only He can satisfy the longings of our heart. So yes, this is your real moment. Say this with me:

Today, I stand in my truest self, unashamed of my journey I've taken to the woman I have become. I am asking Father God to heal my brokenness. I am asking You to help me and remove the confusion that has come to destroy me. I ask for Your eyes to really see people. I ask for Your love to be revealed. I have nothing left and no choice but to totally depend on You for my next breath.

I admit for the first time, in a long time, I am broken and I need help. I need You to heal my heart and the areas that make me weep. Heal those areas of dysfunction that make me like this so that things will be better. I no longer want to try to fix things on my own. I am asking for You to take over. I don't want to help You out; I want You to do it and get all the credit. I don't know what you have for me, but as a WOMAN, I ask for Your will to be done. Thank You for Your presence. I know You are here walking with me. Amen.

Who You Are
The Struggle Is Real

I think the picture we paint for our life is as authentic as we can make it given the information or knowledge that we have at that time. I have found that the more you lean into this question of **Who Are You?** the more you uncover and discover. The onion is always an onion, but the layers underneath take time to peel back. These layers are life's trials, life's bumps, and life's victories that have accumulated over time. These are those things that played a major role in shaping what I call our "identity" or the Picasso of our lives.

Before I dive into my personal definition of identity, I thought I should share how the word is defined in the dictionary.

Identity:
1. The distinguishing character, personality, or characteristics of an individual

2. The condition of being the same yet having something described or asserted that is different from the general grouping.

Establishing Your Identity

We all have the same basic physical attributes and makeup. What differs are variables, some of which can be changed along with some that will never be changed (for it is a branding of who you are as an individual). Identity becomes important because the battle of "who to be" one day to the next is very real.

Who in the nineties did not want to be Oprah or just have a chance to meet her? To have her display of confidence, strength and influence? Who did not love the Cosby family and want some level of success and identity like the family they portrayed? I could go on and on about the things that shape who we want to believe we are, or can be.

Your gender actually announces a large degree of your

purpose and your service to the King of Kings and His Kingdom. Identity rhymes with serenity! When your identity is secured, there are aspects of tranquility and serenity that not only bless your life but bless the lives of those around you.

The hardest part of my journey as a woman was the process of owning who I am. This means embracing the identity of being a woman of many colors. I searched for so many years to identify with who people told me I was, and who they believed I would be, at various parts of my journey. At one point, I was told I would be an evangelist; at another point I was told I would be an attorney, a teacher, and a prophetic minister. All of these titles were of a specific gift, so I found myself on many occasions trying to fit into that description, only to find it just did not fit.

As I submitted myself to a process which I call excavation—the removal of unnecessary debris—that is when I began to understand and own my truest self. It is when you come to the end of yourself that you begin to see yourself for who you really are. We tend to only show people what we want them to believe. As you excavate and peel back the onion, you can see the many layers. As I began to peel away my onion, I began to own the identity of the woman God had made, who had been hidden inside; one which was very flawed, though full of potential.

It was at that moment that I began to see that I am a

woman that God loves very much. And despite all of the experiences that it took for me to arrive at this place, it was OK because His plan was better than the one I had created for myself. At this place, I could look at things clearly because I gave up trying to fix "me" because I was not hopeless—I was just colorful.

Mistaken Identity

If we are all honest at some point in our journey, someone has mistaken us for someone else. My entire life people would say, "Hey, Neesha," who is one of my oldest sisters nine years apart from me. As I got older, instead of correcting people, I would just say hi and pretend like I was her. The problem in mistaken identity is that you cannot receive the full benefits when you operate in mistaken identity.

A case of MISTAKEN identity has sentenced men and women to death row and even the electric chair, simply because they were unable to validate their identity and specific location!

Destiny Principle #1
Know Who You Are!

Destiny Principle #2
Know Whose You Are!

Destiny Principle #3
Know Where You Are Supposed To Be!

Ask Yourself This:

Can you prove or validate your identity? If you were arrested as a **Woman of God***, would you have sufficient evidence to prove it? Would your identity confirm the Fruit of the Spirit in your life?*

Mistaken Identity:

1. To blunder in the choice of (e.g., He mistook her for Susie in the dark)

2. To make a wrong judgement on the character or ability of a person

3. To identify wrongly or confuse with another (e.g., I mistook him for his brother)

They arrested the wrong man. It was a case of mistaken identity.

Somewhere on our journey, we have subscribed to the identity that others have given us and have projected onto us. No longer do we have to embrace the past that defeats us. We can now stand on top of our failure and mistakes and allow ourselves to grow into the person God created us to be.

This is God's purpose for you—that you become who you were called to be, the person Jesus died on the cross for!

- A lack of identity causes us to forget who we are.

- A lack of self-worth causes us to forget what God has done for us.

- Do not ever compare yourself to others. Why? This indicates a need for esteem development or esteem recovery.

- Never allow fleeting feelings of insecurity to rob you of your identity in Christ.

- KNOW **WHO** YOU ARE! KNOW **WHOSE** YOU ARE!

- It is important that we see ourselves the way God sees us and then live in obedience to Him.

- How will you know how God sees you? **He and His Word are one.**

Chosen for the Journey
The Woman Who Is Colorful

Every woman has a journey and a process to walk out in this lifetime. We all have a choice. We can choose to ignore and do it our way or we can choose to embrace and go the road less traveled. As I have shared my very real, transparent journey today, I challenge you to just not settle for the illusion of the woman you created in your mind. Expand your palette to enable the One who actually created you to be the painter, asking for His idea to come through the canvas revealing who you really are and what He has called you to.

To the little girl in you that someone forgot to affirm or validate, I speak to you today and say:

You are **Brilliant.**
You are **Beautiful.**
You are **Called.**
You are **Healed.**

You are **Chosen** to be the woman for this generation to speak life and bring strength to a world that needs you, your scars and your victories.

To the strong colorful woman that have used your career or education to define you, I say to you today:

You are enough. You don't need all of that to define you. You have been created for more than giving, but also to receive love. You deserve love, and God wants to be that first love. You are chosen to be a woman of grace, truth, and one who loves to trail blaze a course for those that need a chance.

To the colorful woman who is lacking true identity and is confused, and has searched for a man to complete you, I say:

- You must know that God knows who we really are.
- Your past does not define your life.
- You must accept that He loves you anyway.
- You must know that God created you for a purpose, and that purpose can be fulfilled.

COLORFUL

Chapter Two

The Wife

Wife, you are colorful.
Your love, your strength, your gift.
You have been chosen for Him!

Deborah

COLORFUL

I Had No Clue;
Just Don't Burn

Wife – you are colorful.
Your love, your strength, your gift.
You have been chosen for Him.

Deborah

Did you grow up hearing the scripture, *"It's better to marry than to burn?"* Well I guess that's all I heard because every boyfriend I had from the time I was a little girl, I said you are going to be my husband. I will say that the mindset of becoming a wife was formed at a very early age, and as I grew older, I realized it was not an optional thing. It was something I needed to do to help me live right.

Deep down, I wanted to live a life that pleased God. Yet I honestly had no clue what being a wife meant, except to love someone and spend the rest of my life with them doing the will of God. I had no knowledge or understanding, except to drive every childhood boyfriend that I had crazy with my idea that they were the one for me. Our ideas are truly shaped as children, and although that idea of marriage may not in and of itself be faulty, how to get there is quite another journey. I knew deep within myself that my childlike idea was of a girl that really just wanted to feel protected and loved by somebody.

So what is a marriage? A Christian marriage is the **union between a man and a woman**. It is instituted and ordained by God as a lifetime relationship between one man as husband and one woman as wife. Well, with me being very creative and witty, I begin to write a list of what I wanted in a husband. Coming from a family that believed in marriage, I just followed what I believed to be true, based on what I saw in front of me. So my husband's list was pretty superficial and not very realistic. It had a few solid and reasonable expectations. However, it was through the eyes of a 19-year-old, and I thought it was pretty brave.

The Church Fairy Tale?

It was a given that my husband would be a man who would go to church, love God, and of course, want to go into the ministry. My ideas on many levels became a list of dreams that I pieced together over time coming from a minister's family, what I called my work of art. The church fairy tale included that we both go to the same church, we meet, and we get married, love God, and live happily ever after. Of course, that's not how this story went, but I had very strong ideals and expectations to live up to. I had a plan and everything had to go within in the time frame and the scope of what I had scheduled. It is interesting how we design and plan, and things seem to be on schedule, not realizing all along that God has something far greater in mind.

Amazing things began to happen, but there was one problem. God's idea was quite different than mine. As creator of a dream that I had to become a wife, the one factor I left out is the man God picked did not have all the same ideas that I had. The journey of God crashing my church fairy tale started. The date I picked—out the door. The man I picked—out the door. The idea of how things would go—well, that was out the door too. Everything was out the door, down to the whole wedding ceremony.

This began a journey of some consistent themes in my life that I will later share as part of my journey of becoming a wife. I am eternally grateful for God's plan being far greater than mine. His plan was much more solid than the one I had in mind. The life of a wife is one of the highest honors you can ever have. If you embrace the journey early on, you will see the blessing from it.

The Wife of My Youth

I have to tell you that the wedding went as well as it could have with all the resistance that was on the scene. I had no idea until 20 years later that I was so high maintenance and shallow on many levels at the young age of 21. As for as being the wife of my youth, I would call her a planner and a dreamer. She had a plan and a dream that she held onto for dear life. Nothing was going to forge or get in the way of that sequence I had created. The problem with this idea or thought process is that I was really saying, *"Yes God, I want you in control,"* but in truth, not really.

This was a harsh reality because I was driven by ambition, wanting to lay the world out before my husband and give him everything a guy could have dreamed. I wanted us to have "the life"— you know, home ownership, two cars, two jobs, and vacations. And don't leave out becoming someone in the ministry together. This is my dream and the life I wanted to create for myself.

I had a plan, and for the plan, I had a plan. In that plan there was no place where I asked for my husband's ideas, input, or even thoughts. I had a DREAM, and I ran with it. This type of ambition has its place but it takes more than one person's drive to work in a marriage. The husband of my youth just wanted to see me happy in all areas, so sometimes, to his detriment, he compromised his happiness for mine. That will get you only so far in life, and something begins to break. I found out that this issue would challenge me later in my life, for I had no idea what was in front of me.

How I saw myself as a wife, was it wrong? After all, I was a girl that had learned to survive because I had to hold on to an idea that *I was* created to become someone to do something of worth or value? My mentor would say, *"Heal the girl so the woman can live."* Well as the wife of my youth, I began a journey that started to quickly crumble and shatter. I could no longer manage all of what had been created. The wife of my youth had to begin to grow up, and needed to operate from a different place than I ever dreamed or even imagined.

The Wife of My Trials

It seems no one likes to go through suffering, or being tested. It doesn't matter who you are. I would say during a strong part of my life, I challenged people to understand their purpose, to understand who they were and who God called them to be. So, what does that really mean when you begin to allow God into the space called, *purpose in your life?* This is the journey of saying, ***"God I welcome You into the reason and the purpose You created me for, and I allow you to finally have Your way in me. I give You the permission to use me for the reason You created me for."*** We can spend our entire lives saying "yes to God, but it is not until we release the reins to say, *"Give me your purpose"* that we find life. When I did this, the trials of my wife life also began.

As I shared previously, this was the one area of my life I felt good about. I am a wife. Everything else has failed me—my childhood, my teenage years, my young adult life. I am a wife, and this has to go right, *right?* So, I put all the stops in place, all the precautions. He loves God, check. He loves me, check. We like each other, check. We have money, check. He is kind of cute, check. All the things I had on my list I could control were in place.

There was a worship song that came out at the time that I played and played. It spoke to my situation, and I found myself at times in tears. The lyrics that stuck out the most were, *"Will your heart and soul say yes, but your yes might cost you everything."* Well, guess what. It surely did! This was the beginning of a series of events that would challenge every idea and every false premise that I had created for my life. I want you to know the launching pad of my freedom came from a simple "yes". But there were also a series of trials that would cause me to place my marriage, my wife title, on the altar and say, "God even though I'm hurting, I want what you want. I no longer have my ideas, but I truly want what you want."

As I began these years of surrendering it all, I began a real affair—a love affair with God—that changed my life, changed my thoughts, and the future of my life.

I began to pray a prayer that went like this:

"God, would You be my romance? Would You be my love affair so much that I can't take my mind off of you? Would You teach me true intimacy? Maybe that part of who I am is distorted. And maybe I never learned how to truly love. There is an area of void in my life that I need filled, and I've been waiting on a person to do it.

Today, I confess, in my own right, that I no longer want to love in this way where I wait on a man to give me something that only You can give. I need that place of a Father and that place of a husband to be filled with Your presence, that it may complete me. I ask that my view of those roles will not be filled with false expectations but what You say about those roles.

Father, place the course of my journey off the areas of rejection and abandonment onto a road where neglect is no longer my portion. I pray now that long life is my portion and that You will satisfy the longing of my heart. Complete me in those areas I am constantly attacked in. You be my shield. You be my breastplate."

This was the beginning of my change. This was the start of my heart truly beating after Him.

The Wife Nightmare

I speak a lot about dreams when it relates to the dream that I had for myself. We all have a dream of some sort, perhaps in being a wife. You love hard, even though you make a lot of mistakes, you hope for the best.

As you grow, you become wiser and learn that the testing of true love is coming. It may not be in the shape or form you would imagine. Most women love from a place that they were loved in or what they believed to be love. I can say that I loved, and as long as you loved me back or as long as you gave, I gave. That stems from a deep-seated place of, *"Do I really trust, or do I love from a place of conditions?"*

There is a true place of frustration that your life reaches where nothing you do works. And, the answer no longer can be managed by your loving, your giving, or any manipulative way. It is the worst nightmare you can imagine. The wife nightmare is when you are finally broken enough to allow God to have your life. The wife that you imagined you could be no longer works and you relinquish all of her to the Father. Let me share some insight on the night this happened to me.

The Night I Called It Quits

I was wracking my brain, saying, "This is too much! I can't do this anymore. I am so tired of the struggle. I am tired of these feelings of abandonment." You see,

36

the pain of suffering feels as if no one understands. When people are stuck in their own pain, yours seems, well, just not that important. This was one of those seasons for me, one I did not choose; it chose me. Well, guess what? I get that everyone needs to draw closer or pray harder or do something. Tonight, I'm not sure that's my story. Tonight, I think I will call it quits.

I quit the fight of feeling inadequate for the journey. I quit the mindset that says, "Poor me." Being up every night until the wee hours can make a person get weary. Meanwhile, I am constantly asking God, *"Hello what is the real deal? Can you speak to where I am? Can you provide some insight to this pain?"*

NO MORE TONIGHT. I QUIT.

- I quit whatever this is that is causing me so much torment and pain.
- I quit trying to figure out what needs to change and what I need to do.
- I quit the discovery of the formula to make things better.
- I quit all this stress that is trying to wipe me out.
- I quit trying to make things better for others; it is His plan not mine.
- I quit feeling sorry for myself thinking I'm the only one that is going through.
- I am asking for some relief, for real, "I quit." I give you these reins. The truth is, this is just a part of

life. No one told me, and I tried to avoid it. I quit beating up on myself because of the choices I made 20 years ago.

- I quit trying to understand people's choices and why they do the things they do.

- I quit the frustration. I am not going to worry about when you will be over and when things will turn around.

- I quit trying to make things better and more peaceful.

- I out right quit trying to see how I can make my marriage, my children, and even me, get it.

- Tonight's the night I quit it all because at some point, all of the things listed above will force you to quit.

- I don't have to get fired from life anymore. I quit. I wave my white flag and said, "I quit."

God, this is Your show. You write the script. You play the next tune because this dance is old and tiring and I don't have the rhythm (motivation) to do this anymore. If You had told me I would be here, I would not have believed you, but I get it. You are not looking for my understanding or my ability to keep going. YOU have been waiting on me to resign from this position and get out of the way so You can be who You always wanted to be in my life, GOD. You don't need my permission or my resume to qualify for this next season of my life.

Help my unbelief in this season. I am writing this resignation letter to all that will read it. I highly recommend that you who are reading this now also resign to quitting the struggle because at the end of the day, after all of the effort, all the plans you make, nothing will go your way until you quit.

So today, I quit so God could be my full-time solution and I could let Him control the deep places of my soul. I never thought I was a person to give up, but tonight, I QUIT.

To QUIT Is Defined As:
- To stop, cease, or discontinue
- To depart from; leave (a place or person)
- To give up or resign; let go; relinquish
- To release one's hold of (something grasped)
- To acquit or conduct (oneself)
- To free or rid (oneself)
- To quit oneself of doubts

This was the beginning and ending of a nightmare. The nightmare was that I felt responsible for the outcome of everyone's lives and took personal ownership for every triumph and every mistake. This was the end of a season of frustration and entering into a season of grace. I realized that God never intended for me to take on such burdens of heaviness nor did He intend on me making everyone pay for the decision that I made to take ownership for the weights of the world.

As I released the wife nightmare, I learned there was a new way to operate—that I could quit and begin to take on a new way of doing things, a new way of loving, and a new way of giving.

Many times we want to quit because we are giving from an impure place, expecting a return that only God can give. Increase is God integrating honor into what is right. As a wife, we must shift our place of HELP vs. HELPER. Most of us live in a nightmare because we are trying to be the Holy Spirit (helper) in our husband's life. The nightmare ends with your new decision to just be a helpmate, not the all-knowing, all-powerful helper. That role is for the Holy Spirit alone. It is when you discover this, that you enter into a season called GRACE.

The Wife of Grace

Do you know you don't know it all?
Do you know you are not perfect?

Do you know you don't have to even understand what's going to happen next in your life? Embracing a life of grace causes you to bow before Abba (Father God) and love your husband from a new place - a place of GRACE. This challenge will cause you to humble yourself and surrender those areas of **unattainable perfectionism** that you created for yourself.

Allowing yourself the ability to become a "grace-giver"

will open doors in your life to receive a helping of much needed grace for your own life. One day, I woke up and realized that as a wife, you are the Helpmate. I can hear so many of you say, *"What does that mean? Why should I relegate to such a position that is so beneath or below me?"* To that I ask, *"Why have we placed such little value on being the helpmate? What is wrong with serving, bringing aid, support or deliverance?"* The first role of a woman or wife in the Bible is that of a Help Meet, which just means someone who helps meet the needs of their husband.

As I mentioned, we sometimes mistake this critical role as something beneath us or demeaning. We need to be more like the Holy Spirit, He is the **Helper** to Jesus. Jesus, is the **answer**, not us. We need to lean into the Holy Spirit to learn how to be like Him.

This Wife of Grace has similar traits to the Proverbs 31 women in that her value is not decreased because of her level of humility or adaptability. (Submission is actually translated to mean ADAPT—the wife is to adapt to her husband, honor, and respect him…)

As a younger wife, I never understood how some women just served and loved on their husband even when I knew the behind-the-scenes situation and his rap sheet. I knew he was not being respectful or truly on the up and up. But that was of no consequence to her, or her joy.

The difference between "her" and me was that I did not have that gift or that joy that she walked in. I realize now that is something I had to seek for to become. To be so secure in the innermost parts of my heart that I understood who God was in me, regardless of the state of my husband. To understand who I was truly serving and where all the grace needed came from. I implore you, younger women and also older women who have yet to grasp this concept, to **give** the grace that you need in your own life.

In my own life, many times I have asked the question, *"SO HOW MUCH IS ENOUGH? How long do I take this or that?"* You see, no one can tell you how much is too much and how little is too little. We must take God at His Word that says, *"But to every one of us is given grace according to the measure of the gift of Christ."* (Romans 12:3)

There also is a lot of truth in that old song titled, *"Just a Closer Walk with Thee."* We have all had our share of striving and fighting, and in our weakness, God's strength is made perfect. However, as we grow closer to God, we find that our fight need not be as we thought. We begin to realize that God goes before us, if we let Him, and He will fight our battles for us.

I love the *Message Bible* because it expresses things from God's Word with clarity, revelation, and relevancy just when I need those areas in my life better defined. This translation makes sure you take a needed "Selah" moment or pause and actually get what God is saying.

Hymn to a Good Wife

Proverbs 31:10-31 MSG
A good woman is hard to find, and worth far more than diamonds. Her husband trusts her without reserve, and never has reason to regret it. Never spiteful, she treats him generously all her life long. She shops around for the best yarns and cottons, and enjoys knitting and sewing.

She's like a trading ship that sails to faraway places and brings back exotic surprises. She's up before dawn, preparing breakfast for her family and organizing her day. She looks over a field and buys it, then, with money she's put aside, plants a garden. First thing in the morning, she dresses for work, rolls up her sleeves, eager to get started.

She senses the worth of her work, is in no hurry to call it quits for the day. She's skilled in the crafts of home and hearth, diligent in homemaking. She's quick to assist anyone in need, reaches out to help the poor. She doesn't worry about her family when it snows; their winter clothes are all mended and ready to wear.

She makes her own clothing, and dresses in colorful linens and silks. Her husband is greatly respected when he deliberates with the city fathers. She designs gowns and sells them, brings the sweaters she knits to the dress shops. Her clothes are well-made and elegant, and she always faces tomorrow with a smile.

When she speaks she has something worthwhile to say, and she always says it kindly. She keeps an eye on everyone in her household, and keeps them all busy and productive. Her children respect and bless her; her husband joins in with words of praise:

"Many women have done wonderful things, but you've outclassed them all!" Charm can mislead and beauty soon fades. The woman to be admired and praised is the woman who lives in the Fear-of-God. Give her everything she deserves! Feast on her life with praises

So after reading and going down the list, we all can find ourselves somewhere in the midst of all that. The theme of Proverbs 31 is that she truly is a WIFE of Grace. She is a woman that fears God and serves her family.

You must receive the grace because it does not come unless you begin to ask for it. Our own gifts and abilities can play tricks and empower us to believe we can do things in our own strength. Yet God's GRACE is available if we allow ourselves to access it daily.

Chosen for the Journey
The Wife Who Is Colorful

So let's have an honest moment, shall we? Have you ever searched the Internet and looked up the definition of a wife and then said to yourself, "*Clearly I don't want to be her,*" or "*This can't possibly be right – she is nothing like who I am.*" Well that is exactly what I did and then I had that question posed to me that every wife in her lifetime will have: *"am I truly chosen for this journey? Am I completely sure?"* The feeling of inadequacy and impossibility swarms the mind. Can I truly be all the things that are required of me? Or perhaps is this another level of my life where God is requiring a deeper surrender?

To be perfectly honest, I did enjoy the honeymoon phase of my marriage, but at this juncture, this next level stuff, well, I could do without. You see, it is in our honesty that I believe freedom comes into play. God shows you your inabilities and exposes the need for Him to invade the spaces that otherwise you would have thought you were fine in. The reality is you are not fine in them, and truthfully, we won't be without God's help.

God chose you to be the wife because He knew that you had just what it took to complete the journey and the womb that could carry many of the promises for your husband's life. Simply put, you are the helpmate, and even though that word in this society, in this day and age, has a negative and nonrealistic connotation because of the many roles women have, it is still possible. You may still ask, "*how am I the one chosen for this journey*"? No one else on earth was chosen to give and encourage the man that God has for you. Your life was uniquely shaped to fit in the plan for his life.

At this time and season of your discovery, your need for God becomes so apparent that you realize you need God to be your first husband. He is the One to totally trust. To place all your needs at the altar and ask Him to help you with that which only He has for you. Yes, although this appears to be simple, it requires deep steps of honesty. To come into the realization that He has given me the ability to carry in prayer dreams and visions for my husband. Something in me has to be changed and transformed in order to be trusted to carry this out.

I can say in this book I may not be able to answer all your questions about being chosen for the journey of a wife. But, I can certainly encourage you to become a true seeker of what God has specifically called you to be in your husband's life. It may not be the original picture you painted for your life. It may need to be white-washed and started all over. It does not matter if you have been married 20 years or three years. The "begin again" is for all of us, especially when we find ourselves not embracing the role that God has called us to in that specific season of our lives.

In taking the Biblical approach to being a wife, there are a couple things that can be said. I actually googled what a wife is supposed to do. Author Barbara Rainey explains this below. I share this because many times as a young woman, we are trapped in the honeymoon phase of our marriage and never live out the true role of Christ in our lives.

WHAT SHOULD BE
THE WIFE'S "ROLE" IN MARRIAGE?
By Barbara Rainey

"Be a helper to your husband.
Respect your husband.
Love your husband.
Submit to the leadership of your husband."

This isn't as hard as it sounds for we should be ever changing, ever growing into the image of Christ. When you realize that you were chosen to be a wife and not a man's mother, it becomes the greatest eye-opener of your life. A mother feels responsible for the outcomes of their children, whereas a wife feels committed to praying, encouraging and supporting. Those are two different worlds. If you have been called to be a wife, it is one of the greatest honors that you have been chosen to do. But identifying the wife in you underneath all the layers of your experience, is your mission.

Wife You Are Chosen For The Journey
Wives - you are colorful and here are a few words to

affirm you as you pursue being the wife chosen for the journey.

- You are the wife God ordained for this man.
- You are equipped with everything He needs.
- You are chosen to birth out the dreams and visions in His heart.
- You are loving, kind, and generous.
- You do all you do unto the Lord so that He may be glorified.

Chapter Three

The Mother

Mother – you are colorful.
You were chosen for this moment to give life,
to cultivate, to pour, to impart into these lives
you have been given.

Deborah

COLORFUL

My Mother

My mother is not only the woman that gave me life, but she showed me the strength of ten thousand men. I'd like to start by saying that she is a woman of grace and a woman that I love and admire. Dr. Maria Crawford is the woman who gave me my **G.U.T.S.,** which I like to refer to as **"genuine undeniable true strength."** She is the reason I know how to fight. I get the brilliance of my mind from my mom.

In my younger years, I never understood my mom. I never understood why she was the way she was. I only saw her fight for us, which challenged me because I did not understand that the true evidence of the love of a mother is that she fights with all her might to ensure that her children have what they need. She cries out in prayer for them to become who they have been called to be.

At an early age, I would always see her every morning on her knees praying constantly. She never missed a day. I had no idea that this would be the ground that I would walk on today. Admitting to you, I never wanted to become my mother because I had an illusion that was shaped at a very young age that went something like this:

- I don't want a lot of kids. *(It was eight of us and seemed like just too much work)*

- I don't want to stay home. *(It just seemed you had no life for yourself)*

The list went on.

When you are immature, whether in age or stage in life, you say many things out of ignorance. What I did not understand is, as a mother, you must surrender to God. You don't choose your path. You don't choose or decide the plan that God has for you. I have to say that my mother taught me to persevere and that I don't have to stand back and just let life happen. She taught me that possibility is unlocked in your "YES" and that your yes may be the hardest thing you have ever have to do.

As my mom would say, "God will be no man's debtor; He will out give you." I am grateful for my mom, and the other moms that adopted me along the way, who showed me a love so unconditional it unlocked my ability to mother.

Mother Avoidance

It's interesting that as a little girl or young teenager, you may say, *"I am going to have this many kids and that is all."* As previously mentioned, I was avoiding being my mom, so I said that I would only have three kids and that is all. I didn't want too many because I wanted to have my career and, of course, travel the world, and so on. We all have done it at some time or another. We express all these things that we plan, or as I described, draw a painting of that we try to fit into the small picture we have created for ourselves. We place clear limitations on the Creator and tell Him, *"This is what I am going to do by any means necessary."*

I really did not understand or come to know what it meant to be a mom until I had my own children.

How did I try to avoid mothering? Well, I had this idea that if I had all the pieces in place, my maternal role would just come—that it really was not a big deal. I could have my career, and I was going to prove it to myself and to my peers that I could be an effective career mom and control everything that happened in my life.

There was something so simple operating in my journey, which I denied every time it came up. I wanted to CONTROL what type of mother I was. I often compared my journey to the women in my life—mothers, aunts, sisters, and friends. I judged their journey to make my journey feel more secure. So many things began to be exposed in my life when someone would challenge my idea of mothering. I would become very defensive and challenged because I did not want to make my life fit into a box.

I have to admit that God had to heal me early on in my life because my teenage years were a wreck. Talk about avoidance. I was a troubled teen. Many things that happened in my journey pointed to motherhood. When I was 17 years old, I became pregnant by a 24-year-old man and the ability to control being a mom started early. I was scared and did not want to disappoint my mom, so I made the worst decision ever. I took a life. I did not want to be a teen mother, not understanding the consequences or torment in my decision. All of that planted a seed of rejecting these things called being a mom. It also caused me to believe early on that I could control my life and avoid being a mom.

Since I opened this can of worms regarding abortion, I have to say this was not a decision that pleased God, and I do not share this with you lightly. As I've grown older, I have spent a good part of my life's mission to stop young women from making that decision because I realize that only GOD CAN GIVE LIFE. I have shared my testimony with hundreds of teens and young women. Abortion is not a way to handle life's hiccups.

As I became married to the love of my life and we began

to have a family, I never knew that becoming a mother would forever change my view on life and alter my journey. I would often tell my husband that each child that came into our lives literally transformed my life. As you continue to read, you will see my journey of being a mother.

The Ceremony

So your life is changed. You no longer have the view that it is all about what you want. You have been transformed, but you decided that you really don't like the person you have become. It was not a part of your perfect little plan, and it does not fit within the scope of what you can see anymore. I was blessed in my younger years to feel I had the ability to have foresight. When I no longer had control, what was God going to do with my life?

After five years of being fired by God and hired by family, I can say that being a full time Mom was never my passion, initially. My passion has always burned deep within me to see greatness and not to fail. The only problem with that is that I left God out on the sideline, saying, ***"I'll let you know when You can add Your part of the plan in."*** So here we are, looking at this whole new life, saying this is not the picture I imagined. Absolutely not. Every girl has a dream in which she wants the story to begin and end. Mine went a little like this:

I will have my education

I will have my career

I will have my husband

I will have my family

I think you can see where this is all going. All the "I WILL'S" made covenant with a picture that God was so merciful to allow.

My pain spoke for a time, those "I WILLS" were the things I saw as a child not work out very well for my parents. Being the passionate creature that He created, "I WILLS" became my drive and determination to maintain a life that in my mind was perfect, but it was not grounded in real life.

Five years later, I am standing here saying, "Wow, God, You changed my life," and it's time to bury the old me that I created and accept the full-time job that You created me for—not the career that I created for myself that was focused on controlling each day with selfish desires. It is a life where I actually have to give each day to the Lord, offering it as an offering unto Him, asking what do you want to do with this day You have given me?

Today I choose to have the ceremony and burn up those idols and the selfishness that caused me to neglect the very thing God entrusted me with.

- **Career Lady**: I lay you down who neglected her family.

- **Religious Lady**: I lay you down who says ministry comes before family.

- **Ambitions (that don't please God) Lady:** I lay you down.

- **Make it happen Lady**: I lay you down. Your gift is only to be used when God says yes.

- **Controlling Lady:** I lay you down. The thought that only you can do it your way must go.

- **Mother that Miscarried:** I lay you down and all the things I could not control.

- **Fixer Lady**: I lay you down and wait for God's instruction, only.

- **Selfish Lady:** I lay down what I think I want and ask God for what He wants.

Today, God, I give you anything that will get in the way of pleasing you that will cause me not to serve you and serve my family with my whole heart. Today I allow God to burn away the areas of my heart that do not give him glory and are not fruitful.

With my whole heart I seek you; let me not wander from your commandments! Psalm 119:10 (ESV)

Picture Perfect - I Can Do It All

I think about the birth of the first three of my children, each one so perfect, so beautiful. As a new mother, everything must be structured so perfectly; no hand-me-down clothes, everything new. I would say I was so particular about everything. It had to be a certain way. This frame of mind will cause you to always be in a hurry, looking for what's next, never living in the moment of life.

It All Falls Apart

Fired By God, Hired By My Family is a book I wrote that you will hopefully read one day, but today, I want to share about a part of my life falling apart due to my concept of mothering.

Have you ever had a bookshelf that was just old and you propped it up against the wall? You may have even put duct tape on the back of it so the books would not fall out. Do you remember that bookshelf leaning up against other bookshelves to stand up until finally the middle caves in and the screws are stripped and can no longer be tightened? It has to be thrown out.

This would describe July 1, 2009, when the bottom fell out in my life and the career and the life that I created for myself ended. I was fired, like for real fired, from what I believed was the one thing that defined me.

I felt I was fired not by my job, but by God that day, and it was to save my family because up unto this point I had no vision for them. I could only see my selfish ambitions and what I was doing to provide and make the life I never had in relation to finances. That day was a true death to what I believed and what I even thought I knew about what was true about myself.

I asked the Lord, *"Why did You have to let it all fall apart? Why could You not just have tapped me on the shoulder and said, 'Change your life'?"* He said, "I did that many times, but you did not have the faith to believe me for what you could not see." There are moments in your life where you can see beyond the illusion that you created for yourself. Many people will come into your life and shed light on your situation, but if you are not careful, you will become offended because you are not ready to receive that it is time for your life to change.

So, what do you do when it all falls apart? Do you sit and waddle and complain that the world has turned its' back on you and yours? Do you let it all fall apart?

When our life reaches a place like the bookshelf where no duct tape or screws can fix it, it is time to scrap what you believed or even knew and lean into a place called surrender. The kind of surrender that follows an experience that has marked your life so that the illusion you created has to die. Your initial reaction may be: I am no good, no one will want me now, I am ruined.

That is the place where everything falls apart.

It was at this moment that I realized I was called to my family, to be the wife and mother that I really never thought I had the capacity to be. The judgement was clouded by the bookshelf that I had created for myself. My priorities had to shift and step out of where I was into a whole new place. Perhaps it is more accurate that I was "kicked out" of the place that I believed my life was called to.

The **SHIFT** is when what you believed about yourself changes and you begin to embrace a place called *"YES Lord"* and where your life truly changes. Your ideas are no longer needed, and you lean into God saying, *"What did You say? Who do you say I am? What is Your plan for my life? How on Earth do I raise these children?"*

You no longer have the answers to life questions, but in the strength of God, you learn the art of letting it all fall apart.

He Wants It All

How on Earth did I get it here? This is the cry of every mother's heart who finds herself in this position. You wake up one day, and you are staring at people who depend on you, who need you to be present. The long-range view looks impossible as you stumble over yourself into getting it right one day and totally missing it the next. I liked to believe that as I started out that I was pretty much in control of things—until that one day I had an encounter that changed me forever.

My god-sister Sophia sent me a song by text, and I actually was home alone, and I hit play and the song was called "He Wants It All," by Forever Jones. As I let the song play, I began to weep. I truly felt **undone** by the words. This song actually caused me to listen very closely to each word as if God Himself was telling me, "I WANT IT ALL!"

So I began to say, "Well, what is it you want?" He said, "I want it ALL." Well, more precisely, at that moment, I heard, "I want that thing in you that believes you can control everything that you told me "No" to.

All of us have inside of us the things we don't want to do—that we don't want to come out of our comfort zone for. It requires total dependency on the Father for everything. I need to clarify where I was at this point. I had three children, and honestly, I wanted no more children at all. I wanted to maintain my illusion, the picture that I painted for my family. The one I created that consisted of this little happy family with three children. I could control it. I could maintain it, and I honestly, at that time, did not want to need God beyond this place.

After the loss of my job, I became controlling over the things I could control. But of course, I was holding onto everything that I believed in my heart I could handle. The thought of additional children was just too much. I will never forget my baby shower with my third child. My sister brought a friend home with her from college, and she pulled me aside and told me I would have six children. At that moment I wanted to strangle this young woman. I said, "I'm sorry. God did not tell me that, and you are wrong."

That day when I was playing the song "He Wants It All," He brought that moment before me and said, "Yes, I want that too." Those are the things that make you tell me what you are going to do and not do. God was asking for a yes that I hadn't given yet. It is not the same for everyone, believe me. What is that thing or idea in your life you don't want to let go of? It causes you to miss the adventure that God wants to take your life on. Being a mom—well that can be an adventure that will deepen your relationship with God. Along the way, you will surrender every ounce of who you are at some point because your children will challenge the very fibers of who you are.

I gave God a *"yes"* and a surrender and I became pregnant with number four. I began to get excited, and anticipated this new arrival, I went to the doctor at 14 weeks, and there was no heartbeat. I was angry and hurt because I could not understand why God had asked me for a yes and now this had happened. What did it mean? Was His plan not true, or was I just imagining this place of total surrender?

I had so many questions—nothing at this point in my journey made sense. And then He spoke, *"Deborah, I am trusting you with this experience of loss because I know you won't waste it. You will share and you will help someone else with it."* Isn't that what life is really about? Not so much what we went through but what we will do with it when it's all said and done? Will I let the loss destroy me or will I allow Him to use it to help impact another life? I can't say that I was I excited about helping someone else through a miscarriage but afterward, I possessed the compassion and understanding of the loss and the challenges of so many women who suffer in silence. It is one of those things that you want to forget and move on from but can't.

At this moment, I told God, "Ok, I tried. I am not willing to try anymore." Seven months later, I was pregnant with my gift, Kylie Julia Grace, a true gift of love.

God will turn your deepest places of hurt and pain into a place of habitation of love and grace. The place called **"I want it all,"** is that place in your walk where you as a WOMAN, a WIFE, and a MOTHER give up your ideas and say, "*I give in to the purposes of God. I give You my life to do as You please.*"

I Surrender - Your Way or No Way

Have you ever heard your mom say, *"Listen here. It's my way or the highway"?* Well that has been much of my journey with Father God. I have come to realize nothing really works without Him.

Children expose your deepest vulnerabilities within and expose your deepest need for Father God. As I have journeyed through motherhood over the last 16 years with six children, the word *surrender* is a word I live by daily.

To surrender is to give in, to let go, to no longer be in control. So, the perfect new mother, with all new things, feels like everything has to be perfect for the new arrival. I changed my babies' clothes three or more times a day with my first child. All the rules we have as brand new moms, right? No one can hold the baby unless they are completely sanitized. No one can keep the child. As the days go on, as a parent you begin to relax as the wisdom and understanding of parenting increases. And you begin to wonder, *Why did I have so many rules?*

Child number two comes along, and you try to maintain those standards, but they slowly start fading. And as soon as number three comes, you realize none of that matters at all. You now have three priorities vs. the twenty you originally tried to have.

These three priorities are:
- Feed when hungry
- Change the diaper
- Nap time

From that place, you began to say, "I surrender," when you are outnumbered, and the control goes right out of the door. The same is true in our lives. We realize God is really the most important priority in our lives. Sometimes, though, it takes trials and stumbling to realize that the things that I could control didn't really matter—the dream I built, the illusion that I created, and the life that resulted began to fade. The more I surrendered to His plan, the more He revealed His ideas for my life.

Now that I am a mom of six, I throw myself at the altar and say, ***GOD I surrender. I don't want to do this without You.*** I understand that all these little faces are watching how I handle issues and consequently, how I respond to life's challenges. It is important I teach them how to go to Father God for everything they need, and I depend on Him to lead and guide them when I can't.

How do I overcome my fear of living a life that I can never control? The life of the Mom is a life you cannot ever really control.

The Deborah in me has moments that still say this is way too much to handle. Who would knowingly sign up for such a daunting task? Then there are moments when I know the reward and the joy that comes when I let Father God take over. He lets me know that I am not alone, that He is walking with me and the road map to being a good mother is written in the scriptures. You see, it is not something people can explain to you, but something you learn in those humbling moments with your children where God lets you know that He holds your beginning and your end.

So, what does surrender look like, and how do you know you have given into God's plan?

Isaiah 55:8 says:

> *"For my thoughts are not your thoughts, neither are your ways, my ways,' declares the LORD."*

Surrender looks like letting whatever ideas or belief you had about life go. Whatever well laid-out plan you had for your family or for being a mom, to give it up. We form these ideas out of different places and spaces. Whether childhood, adolescence, teens, or young adults, all of our experiences shape out two lists in our life— the "I will do this" list. and the "I won't do this" list. We make agreements and commitments to ourselves and tell others to "love me like this" or "be a friend to me like that." Instead, let me take you on a journey of a ceremony called, ***"I surrender all."***

This is that place where you let go and you say, "God,

I just want what you want for my life, and as you lead me, I will follow." It's a place that requires a yielding to a holy and righteous God that renders us totally and completely surrendered to His will and His way. It is where we trust without holding back and leaning on His sufficiency.

As we close, please say this prayer of surrender:

Dear Lord,

Today I will surrender my life to you again. I ask for you to change me from the inside out so that I may know you closer. I give you my family, my children, and all my abilities as a mother. I give you every day of my life and trust you for the plan for my life.

Grace and Mercy Found Me

Who would believe that after this journey, the need for more Grace and Mercy would be required in my life?

We were very intentional about naming all of our children. We believed that a name was an announcement to the Earth who you are to become. Each one of them came with a specific purpose and assignment that also transformed my life.

God, I am so eternally grateful for my oldest child, Jada, whose name means knowledgeable one. Jada taught me that it's ok to not know what to do.

My second oldest, John Wesley, whose name means gracious gift of God, taught me the true meaning of laughter and levity in life.

My third child, Kirsten, meaning follower of Christ, who experienced so many challenges as a baby, taught me endurance and that trouble won't always last.

My fourth child, Kylie, whose name means graceful and beautiful, taught me love on levels that healed my soul.

Then there came a time in my life when I realized in a most unexpected way, that only GRACE and MERCY could have found me.

Proverbs 16:9 (NKJV)

A man's heart plans his way, but the Lord directs his steps.

My story speaks to when you have an idea and plan for your life, but God disrupts it.

After surrendering to another pregnancy, I felt my life was really complete with four amazing kids. On December 1, I was feeling ill, so I went to the doctor, and she recommended I take a pregnancy test. I said there was no way, my tubes were tied. She did it anyway for precaution.

The doctor returned and said, "Mrs. Anthony, you are pregnant." I was in so much shock because that was certainly not on my to do list or even on the new canvas of life that I had painted for myself.

As I rushed to the ER in much disbelief, the ER doctor did an ultrasound and said, "Mrs. Anthony, it's not just one baby. There's an additional sac." I promise I cried at that moment because nothing added up. As months went by and life's tides began to try to close in on my life, God reminded me that He gave me a promise in those two twin girls, which was that grace and mercy will catch you at every turn of your life, and He would not allow me to quit or stumble but would place LOVE in my life that would cause me to keep fighting, keep standing, and keep living.

There were moments after that when I felt like, "God, do you think I am bored and have nothing more to do?" Or did God say, "I pick Deborah Christina Anthony to be the mother of six amazing children, and she can not only handle it, but I TRUST her to be found faithful as a mom?"

On July 6th, two tiny little girls were born, Karis Joy, meaning grace, and Joriah Hope, meaning mercy, and they have transformed the Anthony household to the Anthony 8, and made it stronger and more colorful.

The moment you realize that God chose your life to be colorful and that you can no longer settle for just the picture you created for yourself, and you allow Him to blow on your life with the majesty of his glory there is an explosion of color. You no longer have to settle for what your limited mind could conceive but you can give way to a plan that is far greater than the one you dreamed for yourself.

Never in a million years when I started this journey could I have imagined my life to be so rich, so full. I realize now the younger me in all my ambition was limited in seeing the full color life that God had for me.

Today, I let the younger me embrace the older me. I say that I even though I strive to be a good mother, I will give all six of these gifts back to the Father. I will depend on him to paint his best work in their lives.

Chosen for the Journey
The Mother Who Is Colorful

MOTHER, you are colorful, and here are a few words to affirm you as you pursue being the mother chosen for the journey:

- Mother, God handpicked you and you only to carry that seed of life.

- Mother, the Earth needs what you have so you must give life.

- Mother, you will get tired but take a nap; joy comes in the morning.

- Mother, love with all that you have, even with what you may not have received.

- Mother, you have been trusted to be a vessel to bring forth the next generation with truth and grace.

COLORFUL

Chapter Four

Chosen For The Journey

A Total Surrender Is All a Part of the Journey
Ownership Standing in the Center of Juxtaposition
Owning the WOMAN, the WIFE, the MOTHER.

Deborah

COLORFUL

Chosen

What I thought was so tough was sitting right there in front of me. It took me so long to understand the love of God, and yet it was so simple that even a child could understand. Thank you for challenging me with this assignment. What I realized was my view of love was faulty, imperfect compared to the love from my Father. Before my surrender I had a confused view of how to receive and give love.

Juxtaposition means to place (different **things**) side by side (as to compare them or contrast them or to create an interesting effect) **juxtapose** unexpected combinations of colors, shapes, and ideas— J. F. T. Bugental

This word was one that I learned to embrace as I begin to own all that God was designing in my life, realizing that my journey was taking me on many different voyages that had many different colors. Through it all, God's idea for my life never changed and that I could trust Him, for "He Who Promised Is Faithful." I no longer have to live in shame or in questioning His plan. I can stand tall and squeeze the joy out of life, and never forget to grow and go.

Today, I stand embracing the Father's love. I am free to love Him. I fully accept the price Jesus paid to set me free. I fully allow the Holy Spirit to teach and give comfort in the areas of my life, I never thought I needed. I fully embrace a love that I never dreamed I could experience. My prayer for you is that you also feel the warm salve of healing I have experienced.

As you embrace your life's journey and all that has come with it to bring you to this treasured place in God, know that our God does not waste one ounce of our defeats, victories, or transitions—He uses all of it to cause us to be colorful with all the beautiful bounty of colors that He created.

Isaiah 61:3

*To all who mourn in Israel he will give **beauty for ashes**; joy instead of mourning; praise instead of heaviness. **For** God has planted them like strong and graceful oaks **for** his own glory.*

Deborah Speaking to the Father

I will let You love me!
I have fought You from truly loving me
When You tried to love me to life and living,
I moved out of the way, so I could do it myself!
When You tried to heal my brokenness
I decided I did not need You
SO I tried to heal myself
For the first time in my life,
I WILL LET YOU LOVE ME
I will let You teach me what love is
I promise not to put my own spin on it
or add to it—
OR even try to feel qualified
to receive Your love God

I will let You love me and wash away all that
I tried to create in substitution for Your love
Cleanse my most secret places that I used to cover
up, because of my inability to even
comprehend Your love for me
I give up trying to figure out how much love I need
as if it could be calculated with math
And I give up choosing who deserves my love
because it's no longer my love I am giving
It's Your love that they are experiencing
It is Your love that has carried me
in this place of total surrender

You would rather me be in a place of total
brokenness and feel Your love than to appear whole
And never comprehend
who is really holding me together.

Father Speaking to Deborah

Child of mine,
This is your day where you cross over and truly
experience the reason I shed blood on that cross
for you for so long,
And why I allowed them to beat me so bad
It was that LOVE I have for you
that I paid the ultimate price
It was that love I have for you,
that I will now give to finally love you
It was that love that nailed Me to the cross, and it
was the riches of my love that had Me to get back
UP again so that you would be free
It is that same love that comes in this moment
to comfort you and reassure you
that I want to always love you if you let me
So come on and rest
It's ok to lay back and enjoy the love
I have waited for you to experience
No, there is nothing for you to do but receive
I know that's hard for you to comprehend,
but come on and let Me love you

There's nothing in this place for you to try to
manage, organize, or process.
Come drink from a fountain that never goes dry.
For I want you to **let Me love you**.

Written by
Momma Nina-Marie Leslie RIH
2018

No matter what stage of life you find yourself in as The
Woman, The Wife, or The Mother, I need you to know
you were born for the moment you are standing in
right now.

God took His time and hand-picked you for the season
you are in. When you find yourself in doubt or in
question, slow down and breath; YOU are CHOSEN
for The Journey to be . . .

Colorful.

COLORFUL

www.ingramcontent.com/pod-product-compliance
Lightning Source LLC
LaVergne TN
LVHW021613080426
835510LV00019B/2547